Becoming a GREAT Leader

By,

Daniel Michael Newland

Table of Contents

Dear Leader,

The path is often steep in the leadership journey, and the skies are uncertain. Yet, the most enduring message that resonates through the annals of time is this: Never give up. As leaders, the commitment to our words and actions is not just a choice but a defining character trait. Let the universe witness your unwavering resolve when you promise to do something. When you stand firm against the howling winds of doubt, true leaders are forged in these moments. But what fuels this unyielding spirit? It is the profound realization that the most significant investment you can ever make is in yourself. Your growth, learning, and self-empowerment are the tools that build the foundation of a leader who can weather any storm. When those around you falter, find strength within. Empower yourself, and in doing so, you become a beacon of hope and resilience for others.

Remember, adaptability and resourcefulness are your most trusted allies. They are the silent architects of success in an ever-changing world. With them by your side, there is no challenge too great, no obstacle insurmountable. As you walk the path of leadership, let these qualities be your guide, your companions in every endeavor. Above all, know this—your mind is the birthplace of possibilities, the canvas of your reality. It is not a cage but a horizon vast and endless. Your only limitation is that which you impose upon yourself. Break free from these chains. Let your thoughts soar to the heights of innovation, creativity, and wisdom. For in the boundless expanse of your mind lies the key to your most outstanding achievements, your most enduring legacy.

As you turn the pages of life, remember these words. They are not just a mantra but a compass for your journey. Never give up, honor your commitments, and empower yourself. Your story is not one of confinement but of boundless potential. Let this truth guide you as you carve your path as a leader, a visionary, and a trailblazer in the annals of greatness.

Daniel M. Newland

How To Become A
Great Leader

Introduction -
Becoming a Great
Leader

Leadership capacity is a remarkable ability that calls for ongoing growth and development. Having a title or being in a position of authority is not the only thing that matters; what matters more is being able to inspire and motivate others to work toward a common, shared objective. A great leader possesses qualities and characteristics that distinguish them from others. These qualities and characteristics enable them to create an environment where teams and organizations can flourish simultaneously.

To become a great leader, one must always comprehend the need to enhance personal development and learning. Committing to continuously bettering oneself is necessary to achieve leadership, which is a journey rather than a destination. There are many ways to improve oneself, including actively seeking feedback from others, attending leadership seminars, reading leadership books, and seeking mentorship. Leaders need to adopt a growth mentality to succeed on this path. This perspective enables leaders to view challenges as opportunities and failures as learning experiences.

Having a distinct vision for their business or team is a hallmark of a strong leader. Individuals with this talent can imagine the future and motivate others to strive to achieve that goal. To be considered a visionary leader, one must be able to explain the organization's purpose and objectives in a captivating manner. Great leaders can instill a sense of purpose and direction in their teams by communicating this vision and ensuring they are aligned. This then drives the collective effort. They communicate the vision consistently and passionately, ensuring every team member knows their part in supporting and attaining the goal.

On the other hand, more than having a clear vision is needed. Great leaders also need to have the ability to think strategically. They are exceptionally talented in generating and communicating a strategic plan that turns the vision into steps that may be taken. They simplify challenging objectives by breaking them down into doable tasks, assigning responsibilities, and ensuring everyone on the team is on the same page. To enable their team members to grasp their job and contribute to the broader picture, excellent leaders provide a road map to success for their team members. They regularly assess progress, adjust the plan as required, and effectively communicate changes to maintain everyone's engagement and motivation.

Excellent leaders are not only able to think strategically, but they also have vital emotional intelligence. The ability to comprehend and control one's feelings and those of oneself and others is what we mean when we talk about emotional intelligence (EI). Those who can control their emotions effectively and possess high emotional intelligence are self-aware leaders. They can empathize with other people, have excellent interpersonal skills, and are adept at establishing relationships founded on trust and respect. They are self-aware enough to recognize their feelings' influence on their conduct and decision-making, and they use this understanding to modify their approach in response to various circumstances and different people.

Additionally, effective communicators are among the most influential leaders. They know the significance of effective communication in fostering inspiration and motivation within their teams. They can communicate their messages clearly and succinctly, utilizing various communication techniques to cater to the needs of different audiences. In addition, great leaders can demonstrate active listening abilities, which enable them to offer their undivided attention to other people and comprehend the perspectives and worries of those around them. They provide constructive feedback and create an environment that encourages open and honest communication within the organization. Outstanding leaders can connect deeply with their team members by building solid communication channels and fostering trust and collaboration.

Establishing and fostering a constructive culture in the

workplace is yet another essential component of effective leadership. Extraordinary leaders can establish an atmosphere where team members feel respected, supported, and encouraged to perform to the best of their abilities. They devote time and effort to understanding the motivations, strengths, and goals of the people on their team, and they adapt their leadership strategies to meet everyone's specific requirements. Through the provision of chances for growth and development, the acknowledgment of accomplishments, and the cultivation of a sense of belonging, outstanding leaders motivate their teams to perform to the best of their abilities and contribute to the business's success.

Great leaders set a good example for

others to follow. They are the exact embodiment of the values and principles that they anticiples from their team members. They continuously behave ethically and transparently, demonstrating that they are integrity-driven. They build a culture of honesty and trustworthiness within their organization using their words and actions, ultimately serving as the basis for their organization. Great leaders acquire the respect and loyalty of their team members by leading with integrity. This creates an environment where everyone works to uphold high standards, which is exactly what great leaders want to do.

Strong leaders are aware of the significance of taking care of themselves. They understand that to be an effective leader, it is critically important for them to take care of themselves on all levels— physically, intellectually, and emotionally. They prioritize taking care of themselves and schedule time for activities that allow them to refresh and feel energized. They know they cannot pour from an empty cup and recognize that if they care for themselves, they can provide their team with more assistance and leadership.

To summarize, one must consistently engage in self-reflection, learning, and development to become an exceptional leader. In addition to having the ability to think strategically, emotional intelligence, practical communication skills, and the capacity to create a pleasant work culture, great leaders also can articulate their vision clearly. They lead honestly and set an example for others to follow, earning their team's respect and trust. When individuals invest in their personal growth and well-being, they can create an atmosphere conducive to the success of teams and organizations. By demonstrating these characteristics and beliefs, you can improve your leadership abilities and make an impression that will last on those in your immediate vicinity.

How To Become A Great Leader

Defining Leadership and its Importance in the Corporate World

Effective leadership is essential to the success and expansion of any organization in today's fast-paced and constantly changing business environment. This ability is crucial to the success of any corporation. At its heart, leadership is defined as the capacity to direct, motivate, and exert influence over a group of others to accomplish a shared objective. It is not merely a matter of power or position; instead, it is founded on a mix of aptitudes, characteristics, and an in-depth comprehension of the dynamics of human relationships.

The concept of leadership is highly significant in the business world for several different reasons. In the first place, it is the responsibility of leaders to determine the course of action and the vision for a company. Developing a compelling vision that inspires people to provide their best efforts and light a fire of passion within them is necessary. A powerful and effectively articulated vision is required to bring the organization's entire energy and resources into alignment. This vision also provides clarity and concentration to every individual who is involved.

In the absence of this directing force, a corporation may find itself drifting aimlessly, devoid of purpose and absence of direction.

In addition, effective leadership is a significant factor in fostering innovation and adaptation. Organizations must continually accept new ideas, technology, and trends to maintain their competitive edge in today's business climate, characterized by fast change. The capacity to predict developments in the industry, proactive identification of new opportunities, and the ability to inspire their staff to embrace change are all characteristics of great leaders. Leaders should cultivate an environment conducive to innovation to inspire people to think creatively, challenge the status quo, and investigate new possibilities.

They establish an atmosphere where taking calculated risks is encouraged; failures are seen as chances for learning, and continual development is pursued.

Moreover, experienced leaders can construct and cultivate teams capable of achieving high-performance levels. They are aware that the success of a company is dependent on the efforts that everyone inside the organization puts forth collectively. When leaders are thoroughly mindful of their team members' capabilities, goals, and talents, they can better optimize the distribution of duties, encourage collaboration, and establish a trustworthy and psychologically secure environment. They motivate members of the team to perform to the best of their abilities, in addition to providing the necessary support and resources and celebrating both individual and collective accomplishments. Influential leaders make investments in the growth of their employees by providing them with mentoring and coaching to improve their overall performance, as well as their skills and knowledge.

Leadership is also essential in encouraging effective communication and collaboration among employees within a business. One capable of leading others knows communication is the driving force behind any effective attempt. They ensure that information flows freely across all levels, promoting openness, transparency, and attentive listening. Leaders can facilitate exchanging ideas and insights by fostering debate and various perspectives. This ultimately results in improved decision-making and problem-solving abilities. In addition, they stress the significance of clear and concise communication, intending to ensure that expectations are comprehended, goals are aligned, and everyone is given the authority to contribute effectively.

Furthermore, in addition to these core qualities, leadership is a significant motivator of the organization's culture and values. Leaders serve as examples for others to follow, exemplifying the values and ideals the organization strives to uphold. The activities that they take not only serve to inspire and motivate other people but also contribute to the creation of a constructive working atmosphere that promotes honesty, respect, and financial responsibility. Leaders can influence the actions and attitudes of their teams by constantly sustaining high standards of professionalism and ethical conduct. This helps to cultivate a culture that values trust, cooperation, and high performance across the organization.

In addition, effective leadership has the potential to significantly influence the level of engagement and contentment experienced by workers in their jobs. It is more probable that employees will experience a sense of purpose and devotion to their work when they are led by people who inspire trust and confidence in them. When leaders prioritize their employees' health and happiness and acknowledge their contributions, they create a pleasant environment at work, leading to increased job satisfaction, motivation, and overall productivity. This, in turn, contributes to lower turnover rates and improved retention of top personnel, making it possible for enterprises to save significant amounts of money connected with recruitment and training.

Another benefit of having outstanding leadership is that it assists in navigating through times of crisis or uncertainty. Leaders need to possess the qualities of resilience, adaptability, and the ability to make difficult decisions when confronted with complicated circumstances, such as economic downturns or unforeseen disruptions. The ability of these individuals to retain composure, communicate effectively, and offer unambiguous guidance becomes necessary to keep the organization stable and steer it toward a route that leads to recovery.

Leadership is also significant when shaping an organization's reputation and influencing external stakeholders. Leaders act as ambassadors for the organization, expressing its core principles and ensuring that customers, investors, and the wider community have a favorable impression of the organization. The leaders of an organization can secure strategic alliances, facilitate business possibilities, and improve the organization's overall standing in the market if they cultivate and maintain good relationships with external partners.

I want to conclude that leadership is an essential component in the business sector that cannot be undervalued. It improves employee engagement and work happiness, offers direction, stimulates innovation, produces high-performing teams, encourages effective communication and collaboration, shapes corporate culture, and promotes effective communication and collaboration. The most effective leaders have a singular combination of abilities, characteristics, and a profound comprehension of the dynamics of human behavior. Individuals can significantly contribute to their companies' success and growth by consistently developing their leadership talents. This will result in a positive impact beyond their sphere of influence.

How To Become A Great Leader

Developing Your Leadership Mindset and Skills

Having a title or a position is not the only thing that constitutes leadership; instead, it is the cultivation of the appropriate attitude and the honing of the necessary skills that allow one to motivate and direct others toward achievement. Within the scope of this chapter, we will go more deeply into the essential components of cultivating your leadership attitude and talents, providing you with the resources necessary to become an effective leader.

1. Embrace Continuous Learning and Improvement:

Indeed, great leaders know they are constantly trying to improve themselves. They continuously seek personal development and advancement opportunities through reading books, participating in workshops, or looking for a mentor. By continuously learning, leaders can maintain awareness of their sector's most recent developments, tactics, and insights. They will be more open-minded and adaptable, ready to welcome change, and confidently traverse problems due to this encouragement.

By encouraging information sharing among their teams, leaders can help cultivate an environment that values lifelong education. Not only does encouraging team members to share their information and experiences contribute to their personal development, but it also helps enrich the group's overall understanding of the subject matter. Furthermore, leaders can plan regular training sessions or create opportunities for team members to attend conferences or seminars pertinent to the team's work.

2. Self-Awareness and Emotional Intelligence:

Efficient leaders deeply understand themselves, allowing them to examine their beliefs, values, and feelings. Leaders who have reached this degree of self-awareness can comprehend their strengths and flaws, enabling them to capitalize on their strengths while working to improve their weaknesses. In addition, it assists leaders in determining their fundamental principles, which can act as guiding principles while making decisions and help shape their approach to leadership. With the support of emotional intelligence, an essential component of self-awareness, leaders can better control their feelings and comprehend the feelings of others around them. This ability enables leaders to respond to individuals on the team with empathy, leading to improved communication and healthier relationships. In addition to this, it assists leaders in navigating conflicts and addressing difficult circumstances with sensitivity and tact.

Self-reflection is a practice that should be done regularly by leaders to improve their emotional intelligence and emotional awareness. One way to accomplish this is by journaling, engaging in mindfulness practices, or soliciting input from respected coworkers or mentors. Cultivating empathy with others can be accomplished by practicing active listening, putting oneself in another person's position, and considering others' opinions.

3. Improve Capacities for Effective Communication:

Communication that is both clear and effective is an essential component of leadership. Leaders must effectively communicate their vision, expectations, and feedback to their teams in a concise, motivating, and approachable manner. To ensure that everyone in the team is working towards the same goals, effective communication helps build understanding, alignment, and commitment among the team members.

People in leadership positions should communicate clearly and concisely, avoiding jargon or terminology that is difficult to understand. How they communicate needs to be modified so that it can accommodate a variety of people and circumstances. Additionally, leaders should actively listen to their team members and allow them to voice any ideas, problems, or comments they may have.

Leaders can host regular team meetings, encourage open conversations, and give outlets for feedback to bring about improvements in communication within teams. Additionally, they can utilize various communication methods and technology to bridge geographically scattered teams, guaranteeing that everyone feels connected and engaged.

4. Cultivate a Growth-Oriented Culture:

A crucial component of effective leadership is the establishment of a culture that is focused on progress. To establish an environment that encourages individuals to take chances, embrace learning, and explore innovation, leaders must cultivate an environment. A growth mentality must be fostered throughout the business, allowing each team member to push themselves beyond their comfort zones and realize their full potential. A psychologically safe environment is one that leaders can build to cultivate a growth-oriented culture. This environment is where team members feel safe enough to take chances and communicate their ideas without fearing being judged or facing consequences. Setting challenging goals and giving opportunities for professional development and skill-building are also effective strategies to encourage growth and development within the team.

Leaders can set an example for others by exhibiting dedication to personal development and ongoing education. Promoting cross-functional initiatives and collaboration can further contribute to developing an innovative culture, which allows for the flourishing of various ideas and points of view. It is possible to promote the principles of growth and innovation by offering recognition and celebration for the accomplishments of individuals and teams.

5. Develop a Sense of Trust and Accountability:

When it comes to effective leadership, trust is an essential basis. The establishment of trust among members of a team is a top priority for leaders, who must demonstrate transparency, dependability, and accountability. Open communication and collaboration are made possible by trust, allowing team members to take responsibility for their job.

To establish confidence, leaders need to be open and honest about their decision-making procedures, which include disseminating pertinent information and including team members in essential conversations when it is acceptable. The ability of a leader to fulfill commitments and deadlines dependably and regularly helps to strengthen trust in that leader's capabilities. Self-accountability is a model for others to emulate, and it is essential to remember this.

Leaders must establish an atmosphere that is welcoming and encouraging, fostering collaboration, respect for one another, and teamwork. Strengthening trust within the team further by recognizing and appreciating each member's efforts while fostering a sense of collective accomplishment is possible. The team leaders should also make themselves available to listen to concerns, offer advice, and promote productive talks to increase trust further and build resilience among the team members.

6. Develop Decision-Making and Problem-Solving Skills:

It is common for leaders to be confronted with complex and complicated circumstances that call for an immediate response. One of the most essential aspects of effective leadership is the development of solid decision-making and problem-solving skills. Leaders need to be able to evaluate situations impartially, consider several possibilities, and arrive at conclusions that align with their vision and the organization's objectives.

Through delegation, leaders can empower their teams, enabling team members to take ownership of their areas and contribute to decision-making processes. This can help leaders improve their ability to make decisions quickly and effectively. Leaders should investigate alternative methods of decision-making. These methods include the utilization of data-driven insights, the solicitation of feedback from key stakeholders, and the performance of scenario analysis to gain an understanding of potential implications.

Leadership abilities that include problem-solving assist leaders in overcoming challenges and producing creative solutions. To effectively solve problems, it is necessary first to break down complex issues into more manageable components, collect pertinent information, investigate the underlying reasons, and evaluate prospective solutions. There is a correlation between encouraging a culture of experimentation, learning from mistakes, and developing creative problem-solving skills within a team.

7. Demonstrate Leadership by Setting an Example:

Leaders must set a good example for their team members to motivate them. Because actions speak louder than words, leaders should demonstrate the behavior they anticipate others to exhibit. The leaders of a team acquire the respect and trust of their team members by demonstrating the ideals and ideas they advocate for.

In leadership, for instance, exhibiting integrity in all acts and adhering to ethical standards and organizational values are essential. Leaders must have a strong work ethic, which includes dedication, tenacity, and a desire to excel in their profession. Leaders are also responsible for cultivating an environment that is upbeat and welcoming, emphasizing the need for respect, empathy, and teamwork.

To develop open communication and trust among their team members, leaders need to be approachable and accessible to their team members. Leading by example involves several things, including demonstrating a growth attitude, celebrating the team's accomplishments, and acknowledging and learning from failures. Actively engaging with their staff, seeking feedback and input, and welcoming multiple points of view are all essential behaviors for leaders to engage in.

8. Seek and Provide feedback: Feedback is a handy tool in both personal and professional

development. By regularly seeking feedback from their team members, superiors, and peers, great leaders can obtain insights into their performance and identify areas where they may learn and develop. At the same time, leaders should provide their team members with constructive comments, which will assist them in developing and reaching their full potential.

Leaders should allow employees to provide feedback by conducting regular check-ins, performance reviews, or structured feedback sessions. An open mind and a willingness to learn and develop are demonstrated by actively listening to and responding to input constructively. Additionally, leaders can foster a culture of feedback within their teams, which can help promote continual improvement. When providing feedback, it is not enough to point out areas that need improvement; it should also recognize and encourage positive actions and accomplishments. Individuals can improve their performance and grow their skills by receiving specific and constructive feedback delivered promptly and with support. Leaders are responsible for ensuring that their feedback is actionable, offering improvement direction, and following up to monitor progress.

9. Develop Skills in Conflict Resolution:

Leaders must develop conflict resolution skills proficiently when maintaining a pleasant and productive work environment. Conflict is unavoidable in any group or organization. Yet, how leaders handle it can have a significant impact on the dynamics of the group as well as the overall success of the company.

To be skilled in conflict resolution, one must actively listen to all parties involved, comprehend their points of view, and facilitate open and polite discourse. Leaders must maintain a neutral and impartial stance, concentrating on finding beneficial solutions for both parties rather than taking sides. Efforts should be made to create beneficial outcomes for both parties that address the fundamental problems driving the dispute.

Leaders can also take preventative measures to address future disputes by promoting an environment that encourages open communication, the establishment of clear expectations, and promoting collaboration and teamwork. It is possible to prevent disagreements from becoming more severe and destructive to the team dynamic by establishing platforms for healthy debate and offering standards for conflict resolution.

10. Delegate and Empower: Influential leaders know the significance of delegating responsibilities to their team members and giving them the authority to make decisions. Not only does delegation help to share the responsibility, but it also allows individuals to take ownership of their work and better develop their skills and capacities.

Leaders should delegate tasks per the capabilities and interests of each team member, with clear instructions and expectations being communicated. Because of this, not only is the strain of the leader reduced, but also the team members can concentrate on the areas in which they excel, boosting their confidence and drive.

When you empower team members, you give them the authority and autonomy to make decisions, provide them with the opportunity to take chances, and allow them to learn from their experiences. Leaders are responsible for offering direction and assistance and allowing individuals to develop their ideas and approaches to problems. Due to this, the team will feel more accountable and have a greater sense of ownership.

11. Foster a Diverse and Inclusive Environment:
Understanding how to harness the potential of diversity and establishing an inclusive working environment in which every team member feels

appreciated and respected is essential to leadership. Leaders must encourage diversity in all forms, including gender, color, ethnicity, age, and background. They should also acknowledge the distinctive perspectives and ideas that individuals from various backgrounds might bring.

The leaders of an organization should actively seek out diverse talent and create chances for the growth and development of such talent to promote diversity and inclusion. Within the framework of decision-making procedures, they ought to encourage equality and justice, ensuring everyone has an equal opportunity to contribute and flourish.

Leaders should also advocate for inclusive practices, such as encouraging open communication, actively listening to different points of view, and establishing a secure environment where individuals can freely express themselves without fearing being judged or discriminated against. It is possible to further enhance understanding and empathy among the team members by providing training on diversity and sensitivity.

12. Adaptability and Resilience: When confronted with adversity and change, leaders must demonstrate adaptability and resilience. To be a successful leader, you must navigate ambiguity and accept change. Leaders must frequently make decisions quickly and based on accurate information to deal with unforeseen occurrences.

Being adaptable is being receptive to new concepts, being open to receiving feedback, and modifying one's strategy and plans according to the circumstances. Leaders must be adaptable and eager to learn from mistakes and setbacks to succeed. The capacity to demonstrate adaptability instills confidence and faith in the leader when it comes to the leader's ability to guide the team through difficult situations.

A person's resilience can be defined as their capacity to recover quickly from failures and struggles while retaining a positive frame of mind. Resilience is something that leaders should work to nurture within themselves and throughout their teams. They should instill a culture of learning from mistakes and viewing adversities as chances for personal development. Building resilience within the team can be accomplished by supporting, encouraging self-care, and acknowledging efforts and progress made by team members.

By cultivating their leadership attitude and skills, leaders can establish a constructive and productive working atmosphere that motivates and enables their team members. It takes time and practice to become a great leader. Still, leaders may create a lasting impact and achieve success by embracing continuous learning, self-awareness, effective communication, and other critical qualities mentioned in this chapter to achieve success.

———

Building and Leading
High-Performing Teams

Developing a team capable of high performance is essential to the success of any company. As a leader, you are responsible for recruiting the most qualified candidates and cultivating an atmosphere encouraging productive teamwork, collaboration, and overall productivity. Within the scope of this chapter, we will investigate various methods and approaches that can be utilized in constructing and directing high-performing teams that regularly offer excellent results.

1. Defining Expectations and Laying the Groundwork:

Defining your expectations clearly and concisely is vital before putting together your team. Providing an overview of the team's mission, vision, and goals is essential to ensure that every team member knows their duties and responsibilities. To ensure that everyone's efforts are directed toward the same goal, it is vital to communicate the organization's values and objectives. By providing a transparent structure, you can improve production and eradicate misunderstanding.

Consider hosting a team kickoff meeting to define these expectations. During this discussion, we will discuss the overarching vision of the organization as well as how the objectives of the team correlate to that vision. Communicate the team's goals, milestones, and dates clearly and concisely. To guarantee that everyone is on the same page, it is essential to encourage team members to ask questions and express their ideas.

2. Establishing a Solid Foundation Through Recruitment:

Selecting the appropriate people is the first step in constructing a high-performing team. It is essential to look for people with the required expertise and skills and demonstrate good interpersonal skills and a growth mentality. Explore various viewpoints and experiences to encourage inventiveness and originality among the team members. During the hiring process, individuals should be evaluated based on their capacity to effectively interact with others and contribute to the team's culture.

Prioritize the applicants' adaptability and capacity to thrive in a constantly changing setting and their technical qualifications. Always look for people who have shown that they can bounce back from adversity, are agile, and are prepared to go above and beyond. Consider using evaluations and exercises in addition to the more conventional interviews to evaluate the candidates' problem-solving, decision-making, and teamwork abilities on the job. Setting up your team for success can be accomplished by constructing a foundation with the appropriate talent.

3. Developing a Culture of Trust and Collaboration:

When it comes to developing a high-performance team, it is essential to establish an atmosphere that encourages collaboration and trust. Foster open communication, attentive listening, and empathy among your employees. Cultivating an environment where team members can freely share their opinions, ideas, and concerns without fearing being judged is crucial. When you foster trust and collaboration, you allow your team to work together, find solutions to challenges, and make decisions based on accurate information.

Consider holding regular team meetings, either in person or online, to foster open communication and the exchange of information to foster collaboration. Meetings can be held in person or remotely. To cultivate connections and build trust, it is vital to create opportunities for team members to work together on projects and initiatives spanning multiple functional areas. To emphasize the significance of active listening and empathy, you should demonstrate these behaviors and encourage team members to practice them.

4. Offering Support and Direction That Is Clearly Defined:

You must provide your team with unambiguous guidance and support to lead effectively. Clearly define your goals, ensure everyone knows what is expected of them, and set milestones along the way. Maintain consistent communication with the members of your team and offer direction and assistance whenever it is required. Ensure that your team has access to the resources and training they need to perform their jobs to the best of their abilities. Your team will be able to perform to the best of their abilities if you provide them with the appropriate assistance.

It develops a project plan or roadmap that includes the primary objectives, tasks, and dates. By sharing this information with them, everyone on the team knows the plan and how their efforts contribute to its success. To provide feedback, address any obstacles, and help, it is essential to schedule regular one-on-one meetings with team members regularly. Create an environment that enables your team to produce excellent achievements by actively leading and supporting them in their endeavors.

5. Creating a Positive Atmosphere Within the Team:

Developing a high-performing team requires, first and foremost, establishing a constructive culture inside the team.

Facilitate the development of a sense of camaraderie, the acknowledgment of accomplishments, and the celebration of successes. Cultivating a welcoming and friendly environment where everyone feels appreciated and respected is vital. Encourage a growth mentality characterized by the encouragement of learning from mistakes and the prioritization of ongoing improvements. A team's morale, motivation, and productivity can all be improved by cultivating a positive culture.

Consider organizing team-building activities and events that allow team members to form bonds with one another and get to know one another on a more personal level to foster a healthy culture. Individual and team accomplishments should be celebrated regularly, and their efforts should be acknowledged. Establish a sense of ownership and accountability among the team members, ensuring they have the confidence to take chances and gain knowledge from their experiences.

6. Utilizing Delegation and Empowerment:

Influential leaders entrust their team members with responsibilities and allow them to make decisions. Assigning responsibilities based on each member's specific abilities and interests is essential to encourage team members to take ownership of their work. We will give them direction, resources, and the freedom to make decisions and take initiative. This empowerment increases the team's spirit and allows members to contribute their talents and knowledge to their overall success.

When delegating duties, it is essential to

convey the goals and expectations and provide the necessary instructions and resources clearly and concisely. Having faith in your team members to finish the tasks set for them will enable them to experiment with various techniques and produce their solutions. In addition to aiding and directing along the road, you should encourage self-reliance and personal development while stepping in when required.

7. Fostering an Attitude of Ongoing Education and Growth:

It is essential to foster ongoing learning and development to keep a team performing at a high level. It would be beneficial to offer opportunities for training, courses, and activities that enhance skills. Cultivating a culture of curiosity inside the team is vital, in which members are inspired to learn and develop individually and collectively. The provision of opportunities for growth and development not only contributes to an increase in productivity but also maintains the motivation and engagement of your staff.

Regularly evaluate the training requirements of your team and make investments in professional development opportunities that are in line with the objectives of the team as well as the requirements of the company. It is vital to cultivate a knowledge-sharing culture in which team members are encouraged to share their experiences and learn from one another. Consider creating mentoring programs or buddy systems to foster learning and collaboration among the team members.

Effective leadership, clear communication, trust, and support are required to construct and lead a team capable of high-performance levels. By defining expectations, hiring the right personnel, developing collaboration and trust, offering clear guidance and support, promoting a positive team culture, empowering and delegating, and supporting continuous learning, you can establish a team that consistently delivers excellent outcomes. It is important to remember that allocating time and energy toward developing a high-performing team is an investment in your organization's success.

How To Become A Great
Leader

Hiring the Right People

It is impossible to overstate how crucial it is to hire the right people in today's business environment, characterized by rapid change and fierce competition. The expertise, talent, and commitment of an organization's workforce are the primary factors that determine the organization's level of success. Not only is it your duty as a leader to determine the necessary skills and qualifications for a particular post, but it is also your responsibility to evaluate a candidate's cultural fit, potential for growth, and alignment with the organization's values. Throughout this chapter, we will go deeper into several strategies and methods that can assist you in making intelligent judgments on recruiting.

1. Specify the Qualifications Needed for the Position:

It is necessary to have a complete comprehension of the needs of the job to make educated selections regarding hiring. In addition to merely identifying the title and responsibilities of the function, it is essential to take the time to perform a thorough analysis of the role's scope as well as the primary deliverable obligations. Ask for feedback from those who have a stake in the matter, especially existing employees who could have insightful observations. Consider the technical abilities, competencies, and experiences required to succeed in the position.

In addition, it is essential to investigate how this function fits into the organization's overarching strategy and long-term development objectives. This understanding will be a road map for evaluating applicants and ensuring a successful hire.

2. Write an Enticing Personal Statement for the Job:

It is crucial to have a well-written job description to attract the appropriate people. In addition to merely describing the responsibilities and qualifications associated with the post, you should also use this chance to develop an engaging narrative concerning the organization and the role. It is essential to emphasize the company's mission, values, and culture. A vivid image of the exciting prospects, growth opportunities, and the job's impact should be painted. Please use terminology that can successfully attract the attention of potential candidates and pique their interest. Consider engaging storytelling strategies to make the description unique and exciting.

2.1 Variety of Sourcing Channels:

Sources of talent are now more readily available than they have ever been before in this age of digital technology. Utilizing various sourcing channels to attract the most qualified applicants is vital. There is still the possibility that traditional approaches, such as posting on job boards, will be successful. Still, you should also investigate professional networking sites, platforms specific to your business, and social media channels. Participating in career fairs and forming partnerships with recruitment agencies are two other ways to broaden your reach. You may attract a varied pool of qualified individuals by using several sourcing channels, which allows you to cast a giant net and attract more people. Personal referrals frequently result in high-quality applicants already familiar with the organization's culture. Therefore, it is vital to encourage current employees to refer their contacts to the business.

3. Facilitate In-depth Interviews:

Interviews are essential to the hiring process since they offer the chance to assess a candidate's qualifications, experience, and familiarity with the organization. It is vital to prepare to make the most of the interviews fully. Create a list of questions organized to cover a wide range of subjects, such as technical capabilities, problem-solving abilities, decision-making abilities, and behavioral competencies. When evaluating a candidate's prior experiences and capacity to deal with future issues, it is essential to include behavioral and situational questions in the interview process. Implementing a standardized interview process would ensure that all candidates are evaluated in a manner that is both consistent and fair. If you want to acquire a variety of viewpoints, consider involving a panel of interviewees from different departments or levels within the organization.

4. Determine the Degree of Cultural Compatibility:

One of the critical factors in selecting suitable candidates is cultural fit. Dissatisfaction and turnover are two outcomes that can result from a candidate's lack of alignment with the organization's culture, regardless of how skilled or experienced the candidate may be. When conducting interviews, it is essential to ask questions that uncover information about a candidate's work style, values, and whether they are compatible with the organization's culture. To evaluate the interpersonal dynamics of possible team members, consider conducting group interviews or organizing informal encounters with them. Use behavioral evaluations, personality tests, or cultural fit assessments to comprehend a candidate's organizational fit. Although having technical abilities is essential, having a cohesive work atmosphere that encourages collaboration is even more necessary for long-term success.

5. Consider Utilizing Behavioral Evaluations and Tests:

Interviews do not provide a thorough picture of a candidate's behavior and working style, even though they supply significant information. It is possible to gain a more in-depth understanding of a candidate's personality traits, problem-solving ability, and communication skills by supplementing interviews with behavioral evaluations or tests. A more comprehensive examination of a candidate's capabilities and potential can be achieved through these tests, which can be adapted to evaluate competencies pertinent to the role. Include activities such as simulations, case studies, or role-playing exercises to imitate situations in the real world. On the other hand, incorporating these evaluations into a more comprehensive evaluation process is of the utmost importance rather than using them as the main factor in determining whether to hire someone.

6. Verify Personal References and Conduct Background Investigations:

In the process of hiring new employees, it is essential to check the references of candidates and to investigate their backgrounds thoroughly. You should contact their previous employers or professional contacts to learn more about a candidate's work ethic, performance, and collaboration capacity. It is essential to confirm that their qualifications, accomplishments, and professional ties are accurate. In addition, it is vital to conduct thorough background checks to guarantee no hidden problems or warning signs that could negatively affect a candidate's suitability for the post. You should always follow all applicable legal rules and privacy policies throughout this procedure.

7. Involve the Most Important Stakeholders:

The decisions made about hiring significantly impact a business's performance, and it is essential to involve critical stakeholders in the employment process. These stakeholders may consist of members of the team who will be engaged in close collaboration with the newly hired employee, senior leaders who oversee the department, or representatives from across functional areas. Inquire about their thoughts and opinions regarding the necessary abilities, cultural experience, and team dynamics. Their feedback should be considered part of the decision-making process because their views can provide valuable perspectives and boost the likelihood of a successful hire. As an additional benefit, including stakeholders in the interview process can facilitate the development of a sense of ownership and camaraderie among the team members.

8. Determine the Level of Potential for Growth:

Evaluating a candidate's existing abilities and qualifications is critical; nevertheless, it is equally important to analyze their potential for advancement. It is essential to go beyond the immediate job requirements and consider a candidate's capacity and willingness to learn, adapt, and grow within the organization. Be sure to evaluate their adaptability, problem-solving abilities, and desire to absorb feedback. By looking for indicators, determine whether they are willing to take on new tasks and are open to continual learning. It is possible to ensure that your organization is future-proofed and to develop a dynamic and innovative culture by hiring individuals with growth potential.

9. Consider Diversity and Inclusion:

Diversity and inclusion are imperatives for any forward-thinking organization. Actively seek to build a diverse workforce by casting a wide net and considering candidates from different backgrounds, cultural experiences, and perspectives. Challenge any unconscious biases during the selection process and promote a fair and objective assessment of candidates. Encourage inclusivity by creating an environment where diverse voices are heard and valued. Foster a workplace culture that celebrates and appreciates diversity, enabling the organization to benefit from various talents, ideas, and perspectives.

By incorporating these strategies and techniques into your hiring process, you can enhance your chances of finding and hiring the right people who will contribute to your organization's success and foster a collaborative and thriving work environment. Remember, hiring is not solely about technical skills; it is about selecting individuals who align with the company's values, possess a growth mindset, and have the potential to make a lasting and positive impact on the organization's journey toward success.

How To Become A Great Leader

Effective Communication

In today's fast-paced and constantly changing business environment, communicating effectively has emerged as one of the most important abilities for a leader. When it comes to their motivation, productivity, and general success, how you communicate with your staff can make or break their success. As a leader, you must motivate and inspire your team members with the words and actions you choose to use.

1. Effective Communication and Active Listening:

One of the most critical components of effective communication is active listening. It is not enough to hear the words stated; one must also genuinely comprehend the meaning and the feelings that lie under the surface. When you are in a leadership position, it is crucial to provide a secure and encouraging atmosphere in which everyone feels heard and respected. Take the time to participate in conversations fully, keep eye contact with the people you are talking to, and demonstrate a genuine interest in what the other members of your team have to say. Participating in active listening allows you to acquire valuable insights and viewpoints and helps you cultivate a culture of trust and respect within your team.

2. Providing Instructions That Are Both Clear and Concise:

In terms of communication, clarity is of the utmost importance. The team members may experience uncertainty and a loss of motivation if there is ambiguity. It is essential to ensure that your directions are clear, concise, and easy to grasp for everyone involved, whether delegating duties or creating goals.
Put complicated ideas into terms that are easy to understand, and make sure to establish objectives that are both specific and measurable. This will ensure that there is no

space for misunderstanding. Eliminating ambiguity is a great way to set your team up for success and allow them to work together toward a common goal while having a clear grasp of the responsibilities assigned to them.

3. Adapting Your Communication Style:

When it comes to communication, influential leaders are aware that no one-size-fits-all solution works for everyone. Personalities, communication styles, and the things that motivate people are all unique to everyone. To inspire and encourage your team, it is essential to modify your communication style to be appropriate for each individual and the current scenario. Certain members of the team may respond positively to communication that is direct and assertive. At the same time, others may flourish in an environment that is more supportive and collaborative. You may effectively motivate and inspire everyone by tailoring your communication approach to their preferences if you have a thorough awareness of the preferences of your team members.

4. The Power of Positive Reinforcement:

The use of positive reinforcement is an effective method for stimulating motivation and constructing a robust culture within a team. Honor and celebrate your team's accomplishments, no matter how big or small they may be. It is possible to instill a sense of pride and motivation inside the team by recognizing the efforts and achievements of every individual member. In addition, offer constructive direction and constructive critique for improvement. When you aid and provide directions, you help to cultivate an environment that values ongoing education and development. It is beneficial to your team members to encourage them to expand their skills and capabilities since this will lead to increased motivation and better production.

5. The Importance of Transparency in Difficult Circumstances:

When faced with difficulties or interruptions, effective communication becomes much more critical than it already was. To be an effective leader, it is essential to interact with your team openly and honestly. Communicate the situation publicly and honestly, discuss potential solutions, and include your team members in decision-making during the correct times. Because of your honesty and your ability to persevere through challenging situations, your team will appreciate you. You can create a space where your team feels appreciated and supported by cultivating an attitude of trust and transparency. Thanks to the space you have created, this will allow them to conquer challenges together.

6. The Craft of Storytelling:

Stories can link people with one another. Leverage the power of narrative to encourage and inspire your team to achieve their goals. It is important to share success stories and examples of individuals or teams who have triumphed over challenges and produced extraordinary achievements. Construct narratives that emphasize the difficulties encountered, the methods utilized, and eventual success. By visualizing these tales, you motivate your team members to believe in their capabilities and strive for accomplishment. In addition to fostering emotional ties and imparting a sense of purpose, stories are a powerful source of motivation and inspiration for action. Communication is not only about what you say but also about how you express it.

7. Non-Verbal Communication:

Communication is about more than what you say. Body language, tone of voice, and facial expressions are all examples of non-verbal communication tactics that can potentially transmit powerful messages. It is essential to keep your body language open and approachable, speak positively and passionately, and pay attention to the expressions on your face. How your message is perceived is significantly influenced by these non-verbal clues. You will be able to build a communication style that is genuine and compelling, which will resonate with your team if you align your non-verbal communication with your spoken message.

8. Understanding and Managing Emotions:

Regarding effective communication and leadership, emotional intelligence is an essential skill. It entails being able to comprehend and control your feelings, as well as being able to empathize with other people's feelings. Your ability to manage difficult situations with coolness and objectivity while providing an excellent example for your team directly correlates to your ability to recognize and control your emotional responses.

Additionally, strengthening bonds and trust among members of your team can be accomplished by empathic listening and acknowledging the feelings that they are experiencing. The team members experience increased motivation and productivity when they feel understood and supported.

9. Establishing a Personal Connection:

Establishing rapport with the people on your team is necessary for effective communication. Please get to know them and understand their capabilities, limitations, and goals. Make it clear that you are genuinely interested in their lives, ask questions with open-ended answers, and actively participate in conversations beyond themes linked to work. To establish a sense of belonging and mutual respect among your team members, you should cultivate personal ties with them. This relationship improves communication, making engaging and inspiring your team more straightforward while working toward accomplishing shared objectives.

10. Seek Feedback:

When you are in a leadership position, it is necessary to adopt a growth mentality and consistently seek Feedback from your team. Maintain a state of attentive listening and remain receptive to criticism, comments, and ideas for enhancement. You should encourage the members of your team to voice their opinions, and you should also give opportunities for open communication and discussions whenever possible. You can establish an environment conducive to collaboration by adopting constructive Feedback, demonstrating that you valuc the thoughts and ideas of the individuals involved. Not only does continuous improvement increase communication, but it also gives your team the ability to continuously develop and innovate without stopping.

In conclusion, effective communication is a talent that is vital for any leader who wants to inspire and motivate their team. Engaging in active listening, providing clear instructions, adjusting your communication style, providing positive reinforcement, being transparent during difficult times, employing storytelling, paying attention to non-verbal cues, cultivating emotional intelligence, building rapport, and seeking continuous improvement are all ways in which you can create a powerful and motivated team that achieves remarkable results. Communication serves as the basis upon which great teams are constructed. It enables individuals to perform to the best of their abilities and allows the team to achieve new levels of success.

How To Become A Great Leader

―――――

Driving Growth and Innovation as a Leader

When achieving long-term success in today's continuously changing business environment, it is essential to concentrate on growth and innovation. As a leader, you are tasked with motivating and cultivating a culture inside your organization that is entirely inventive and has forward-thinking initiatives. This chapter provides a thorough guide that will assist you in navigating the obstacles and opportunities in this dynamic environment. It explores various techniques and approaches leaders may utilize to create growth and Innovation.

1. Adopt a Growth Mindset:

A growth mindset is an essential quality for fostering growth and Innovation. As a leader, you must nurture and encourage this mindset among your team members. Individuals who have a growth mindset are those who feel that their skills and intelligence may be improved with the application of sufficient effort and dedication. Create an atmosphere conducive to Innovation by encouraging people to adopt a growth mindset.

By establishing stretch goals that push the limitations of your team while simultaneously giving the necessary support, you may encourage them to embrace challenges. It would help if you encouraged them to continue in the face of setbacks and to consider failures as great lessons and possibilities for growth and learning via the process of failing. By cultivating a growth mindset, you increase your capacity for resilience and promote continual improvement.

2. Encourage Cross-functional Teams and Collaboration:

Fostering growth and innovation frequently calls for the participation of several individuals and the incorporation of various points of view. It is vital to foster collaboration by providing opportunities for teams from different functional areas to collaborate on projects. One way to encourage innovation is to bring together individuals from different departments to interact with one another and share their unique perspectives and areas of expertise.

Establish channels through which team members can communicate their perspectives, offer their thoughts, and work together to solve problems. It is essential to encourage kids to participate in constructive debates, question the status quo, and look for other points of view. You may harness the collective intelligence and creativity within your business by cultivating a culture of collaboration, ultimately leading to the development of ground-breaking inventions.

3. Establish a Culture That Encourages Experimentation:

Establishing a culture that encourages

experimentation is crucial to propelling growth and innovation within the organization. You should provide your staff with the ability to experiment with new ideas, try out different techniques, and take risks that are well thought out. Providing the required resources, time, and support is vital to facilitate experimenting.

Motivate people to adopt a mentality that views failure as a necessary step toward achievement. To achieve continuous improvement, you should encourage your team members to share the lessons they have learned from their experiments, regardless of the results. Celebrate both the successful experiments and those that did not provide the expected results, as both types of experiments can generate valuable insights that can be used for future undertakings. You can foster an environment conducive to innovation by providing a secure environment where people can experiment.

4. Encourage a Culture of Learning:

Learning culture is essential for fostering

growth and innovation in an organization. In addition to providing opportunities for professional development, it is necessary to encourage ongoing learning. This can involve giving staff opportunities to participate in training programs and workshops or sending them to industry conferences and events. Because you are investing in the growth and development of your team, you are giving them the ability to bring new ideas and unique ways of thinking to the table.

Encourage sharing information and establish forums where employees can discuss their learning and experiences. Create mentorship programs where more experienced workers can guide and mentor less experienced staff members. To facilitate the exchange of ideas and information, you should encourage your team members to pursue personal growth and learning in areas that are outside their areas of expertise.

5. Establish Clearly Defined Objectives and Encourage:

Accountability To effectively promote development and innovation, it is essential to establish clearly defined objectives and ensure that your team is held accountable for their performance. Communicate the vision and goals of your organization clearly and concisely and collaborate with your team to devise plans that can be implemented to attain those goals. It is helpful to break down larger goals into more attainable targets to provide a sense of direction and progress.

To ensure that everyone is on the same page and focused on driving growth, it is essential to have regular reviews of progress and to provide constructive criticism. It is vital to cultivate a culture of accountability in which individuals take responsibility for their actions and achieve results. To keep one's enthusiasm and momentum going, it is important to celebrate milestones and victories along the route.

6. Remain Current on Market Trends and Emerging Technologies:

As a leader, it is essential to remain current on the most recent market trends and emerging technologies that have the potential to influence your business. Maintain up-to-date industry knowledge, keep yourself informed by attending conferences and seminars, aggressively network with other leaders, and urge your team members to do the same.

You can maintain your relevance in the industry and anticipate the changing needs of your customers by investing in market research and doing regular competitive evaluations. To acquire a more comprehensive understanding, you should encourage your team to discuss market insights and investigate the possibility of forming partnerships or working with external stakeholders. You can discover new prospects for growth and innovation if you stay ahead of the curve and the competition.

7.Create a Risk-Tolerant Environment:

It is often necessary to take chances to drive growth and innovation, and it is essential to cultivate a risk-tolerant environment. When you are in a leadership position, it is necessary to cultivate an atmosphere in which taking measured risks is encouraged. Encourage your team members to produce daring and ambitious ideas without fearing failure. If things do not go according to plan, offer encouragement and do not remember and learn from victories and mistakes.

It is essential to provide a secure and encouraging environment where team members may freely express their thoughts and share their suggestions for creative solutions. Cultivating a culture where errors are seen as learning opportunities is necessary, as this environment will encourage ongoing progress and growth.

8.Celebrate and Reward Innovation:

Within your organization, it is essential to acknowledge and celebrate creative ideas and activities that have produced positive results. It is necessary to cultivate a culture that recognizes and appreciates innovation. Acknowledging individuals on the team who contribute to innovation publicly is essential. This can be done through internal communication channels, team meetings, or events for the entire organization.

Consider instituting reward programs or financial incentives for exceptional inventive accomplishments. Through the implementation of peer recognition programs, staff should be encouraged to work together, and acknowledgment should be given for innovative efforts. Creating a culture that supports and promotes growth and innovation can be accomplished by demonstrating respect for innovative ideas. One of the most important things you can do as a leader to ensure the long-term success of your organization is to drive growth and innovation. With the adoption of a growth mentality, the promotion of cooperation, the creation of space for experimentation, the cultivation of a learning culture, the establishment of clear goals, the maintenance of an informed attitude, the cultivation of an environment that is risk-tolerant, and the celebration of invention, it is possible to build an atmosphere that helps growth and innovation flourish.

It is essential to keep in mind that, as a leader, you possess the ability to motivate and propel the change that is essential for your organization to maintain its competitive edge and prosper in a business environment that is constantly shifting. You allow your team to achieve new heights and seize possibilities for sustainable success by implementing these ideas and cultivating a culture that encourages growth and creativity.

How To Become A Great Leader

Managing Conflict and Overcoming Challenges in the Workplace

A leader must possess the ability to handle conflict and navigate complex situations effectively. Conflict is inherent in any workplace; a leader must possess these talents. In this chapter, we will go deeper into various strategies and approaches that can assist you in addressing issues and overcoming hurdles to create a harmonious work atmosphere conducive to collaboration.

1.Comprehend the Causes of Conflict:

It is essential to have a solid understanding of the various causes of disputes to handle them effectively. The differences in attitudes, values, or beliefs that exist between individuals can give rise to conflicts.

Conflicts can also occur due to personal or professional conflicts, power struggles, competition for resources, or structural challenges within the organization. You can establish specific solutions for conflict resolution if you first identify the underlying causes of the disagreement.

2. Fostering an Attitude of Open Communication:

To successfully resolve conflicts, open and honest communication is essential. Encourage team members to be open and honest about their opinions and concerns to cultivate an environment characterized by trust and respect. Allow for regular feedback and debate to take place through venues such as team meetings, one-on-one sessions, or anonymous suggestion boxes. It is essential to pay attention to all parties involved and try to comprehend their points of view and interests. Ensure that everyone has the impression that they have been heard and considered.

3. Fostering Cooperation and a Willingness to Make Compromises:

Promoting collaboration and the pursuit of compromise can result in outcomes that benefit both parties involved in a conflict. Rather than focusing on individual interests, encourage team members to concentrate on the team's overall objectives to cultivate a culture of shared responsibility. It is crucial to facilitate brainstorming sessions that stimulate divergent thinking to facilitate the development of novel and creative alternatives. Motivate people to be adaptable and willing to make concessions, which can result in more harmony and cooperation and should be encouraged. When trying to find beneficial solutions for both parties, it is helpful to employ strategies such as interest-based bargaining, which involves the parties concentrating on their fundamental interests rather than taking dogmatic positions.

4. Methods Utilized for the Resolution of Conflicts:

It is vital to employ mediation or other approaches to conflict resolution to resolve complex issues. If you are in a position of authority, you can arrange mediation sessions, which involve establishing a neutral setting where all parties can voice their concerns. To steer the resolution process effectively, it is vital to become familiar with various approaches to conflict resolution. Some of these techniques include active listening, reframing, and establishing consensus. Whenever necessary, seek the assistance of skilled mediators or professionals specializing in dispute resolution.

5. Addressing Toxic Behaviors:

Toxic behavior in the workplace can hurt a team's dynamics, which can exacerbate conflicts. To maintain a healthy work environment, it is essential to confront behavior of this nature as soon as it occurs. In addition to establishing clear standards for acceptable behavior, you should implement a zero-tolerance policy for bullying, harassing, or disrespectful behavior. To address toxic conduct and ensure that everyone feels safe, respected, and valued, it is necessary to take the right actions, such as coaching, counseling, or punitive penalties. It is crucial to foster a culture of pleasant interactions among team members. Therefore, it is critical to encourage the development of emotional intelligence, empathy, and self-awareness.

6. Establishing a Culture of Trust and Transparency:

The underlying elements of trust and transparency facilitate the resolution of conflicts and the triumph over obstacles. Establishing a culture at work that promotes trust, open communication, and constructive criticism is essential. Share information openly and honestly, ensuring all team members are updated on any decisions or organizational changes that may affect them. It is vital to cultivate an environment where errors are regarded as chances for learning and where blame is replaced with accountability and support. To reinforce a pleasant work environment, it is essential to recognize and reward actions that encourage trust, teamwork, and effective dispute resolution.

7.Getting Knowledge from Difficulties:

Opportunities for growth and development can be found amid challenges and disputes. It is essential to encourage your team members to perceive obstacles as opportunities for personal and professional development and learning experiences. Encourage employees to increase their problem-solving abilities, resilience, and flexibility by supporting them in working toward a growth mindset. Establish a secure setting where errors are seen as chances for growth and development and encourage them to be taken seriously. Encourage sharing information and the ongoing acquisition of new skills by implementing training programs, mentoring, and cross-functional projects.

8. Attempting to Advance One's Professional Career:

Continual development is necessary for leadership qualities, particularly in managing internal conflicts. To improve your skills in conflict resolution, you should look for opportunities to participate in professional development programming.

Participants should participate in leadership programs, workshops, or seminars centered on approaches and strategies for conflict resolution. You need to self-reflect to find areas where you could improve your ability to manage disputes and overcome problems. Continually focus on improving your skills in conflict management and developing your capacity to navigate and conquer problems in the workplace effectively. Consider getting a conflict resolution certification or enrolling in advanced classes to expand your knowledge and expertise.

In conclusion, the ability to effectively manage conflict and triumph over problems in the workplace is an essential skill for any leader. To create a work environment that is conducive to growth, productivity, and success, it is necessary to have an understanding of the various sources of conflict, promote open communication, facilitate collaboration and compromise, address toxic behavior, foster transparency, and trust, embrace challenges as learning opportunities, and seek ongoing professional development. It is important to remember that resolving conflicts is an ongoing process that calls for devotion, empathy, and a commitment to cultivating positive connections among your team members. To cultivate a culture in your organization characterized by understanding, collaboration, and accomplishment, you must take the initiative to handle issues and overcome problems.

How To Become A Great Leader

Developing Your Leadership Brand

For aspiring leaders, constructing a robust and indisputable leadership brand is becoming increasingly important. Your leadership brand is not limited to your reputation; it incorporates the perceptions of others, the values you maintain, and the distinctive attributes you bring to the table. Developing a powerful leadership brand not only differentiates you from other individuals but also leaves an indelible mark on your team, organization, and the sector in which you operate. To comprehend that establishing your leadership brand is not a one-time exercise but rather an ongoing process that requires thorough introspection, consistent alignment, and purposeful action, it is essential to have this understanding before beginning this path that will impact your life.

To lay the groundwork for developing a leadership brand, it is essential to comprehend your unique values and strengths. Your natural leadership style is reflected in these fundamental values and distinguishing attributes, which also serve as the guiding principles that direct the development of your brand. Spend some time thinking about the reasons that motivate you to act in a certain way, the qualities that define you as a leader, and the kind of impact you hope to have on the world. Through the process of establishing your unique selling proposition, you can start the process of developing a leadership brand that accurately reflects who you are.

Not only should you think about what is important to you while determining your values, but you should also think about how these values interact with your team and company's requirements and anticipated outcomes. It is essential to look for areas of alignment and synergy because doing so will help cultivate a feeling of shared purpose and boost your capacity to lead effectively. Creating a healthy and inspiring work culture that fosters individual growth and teamwork may be accomplished by first gaining knowledge of your team's underlying motivations and then matching those motivations with your values.

After elucidating your values and strengths, the subsequent stage matches them with the organization's vision, mission, and values. It is not appropriate for your leadership brand to operate in a vacuum; rather, it should be an extension of the organization's brand and the company's ultimate goals. Your commitment to the organization is strengthened due to this alignment, which gives clarity and consistency to your team and the stakeholders we serve. Establishing trust and credibility generates a feeling of purpose that brings everyone together to pursue a common goal.

Make sure you are aligned by paying

attention to the culture and values already present in your organization. It would help if you investigated how your brand might contribute to and improve these features. Understanding the organization's strategic objectives, long-term goals, and desired outcomes is essential. Acquiring this knowledge will make it possible for you to position your leadership brand in such a way that it perfectly aligns with the business's overarching goals. This will enable you to lead effectively and have a significant influence.

Action that is both consistent and intentional is a crucial component in the process of developing an effective leadership brand. To merely preach particular principles or assert that you possess leadership traits is not sufficient; you must also actively display these qualities via your choices, actions, and words you choose to employ. Leadership that leads by example is of the utmost importance because it establishes the standard for the entire organization and motivates others to follow in its footsteps. Integrity should be embodied, obligations should be fulfilled, and constant loyalty to your brand should be maintained. A powerful leadership brand is built on authenticity; people can instantly recognize when someone is not sincere. A genuine reflection of who you are should be included in your leadership brand. This will make it easier to cultivate trust and meaningful connections with others.

In addition to exhibiting your ideals and values, you should acknowledge the power of engaging in effective communication. Your vision should be articulated noticeably and consistently, and you should explain the "what" and the "why" behind your decisions and actions. This openness and transparency results in a sense of trust and comprehension among your team members, which in turn helps to cultivate a collective dedication to the organization's objectives. Additionally, active listening is a component of effective communication. To demonstrate empathy and a desire to consider various points of view, it is essential to solicit feedback and sincerely listen to other people's perspectives. Your leadership brand will be strengthened due to this inclusivity, and your dedication to growth and collaboration will also be strengthened.

Developing your leadership brand involves more than just taking specific actions; it also creates solid relationships and a massive network. Investigate the possibility of establishing connections with other leaders, not only within your organization but also in the industry. Having meaningful conversations, working together on projects, and actively participating in industry events, conferences, and committees arc all aspects of your professional life. Your credibility and influence will increase, and you can access new opportunities if you establish yourself as a thought leader. You can amplify your leadership brand by harnessing collective strengths and shared aspirations when you form alliances with individuals within your organization who share similar values and beliefs.

It is not simply about furthering your agenda. It would be best if you focused on developing contacts and networking. A more appropriate strategy would be to approach it with a genuine desire to learn from others, share expertise, and contribute to expanding your sector. Establishing yourself as a leader dedicated to ongoing learning and growth can be accomplished by active participation in communities, professional associations, and mentorship programs. As a support system, these relationships offer you valuable insights, guidance, and possibilities for cooperation, all of which have the potential to build your leadership brand further.

In the modern period, online platforms and publications specific to a particular industry have emerged as effective methods for enhancing a leadership brand. Participate in social media events to share your knowledge, experiences, and thoughts with others.

Building a professional online presence that is in line with your brand and continuously provides value to your target audience is something you should strive to accomplish. Please pay close attention to the message you communicate across all these channels, ensuring that it accurately reflects your leadership brand and strikes a chord with the people you wish to reach. It does not matter what media you choose to communicate through; what matters is that you consistently maintain professionalism and authenticity.

Maintaining a commitment to learning and development is necessary to refine and develop your leadership brand continuously. Maintain a current awareness of the latest developments and trends in the business, prioritize engaging in ongoing personal and professional development, and get input from mentors, peers, and team members. Recognize feedback as a chance for personal growth and improvement and allow it to influence positively how you present yourself as a leader. Instilling a culture of feedback among your team helps to cultivate an atmosphere of trust and progress, which in turn motivates people to contribute to their leadership journey as well as your own.

To summarize, establishing your leadership brand is an ongoing process that involves various aspects and calls for profound reflection, consistent alignment, and deliberate action. When you invest in your leadership brand, you not only differentiate yourself as a leader but also motivate other people, spark change, and leave an indelible mark on your team, company, and industry. Embrace this transforming journey, recognize the iterative nature of it, and allow your leadership brand to thrive so that you can leave an everlasting impression on the world.

How To Become A Great Leader

Achieving Long-Term Success as a Great Leader

Becoming a great leader is not a destination; it is a journey that lasts a lifetime and involves ongoing growth and development. Throughout this book, we have discussed various areas of leadership, emphasizing the essential characteristics and methods necessary to become an effective leader. In this final chapter, we go further into the crucial components required for establishing long-term success as a great leader.

1.Embrace the Concept of Lifelong Learning:

A great leader is aware that the quest for knowledge and learning is an endeavor that never ends. They understand that the key to achieving true wisdom is maintaining an open mind to new ideas, points of view, and experiences. They are always looking for new ways to broaden their knowledge base, whether through reading large amounts of material from various genres, attending conferences and workshops, taking part in online courses, or having meaningful talks with professionals in their field. Exceptional leaders maintain relevance, inventiveness, and adaptability by searching out new information and unique perspectives in a constantly evolving world.

2.Cultivate Emotional Intelligence:

Emotional intelligence is a skill that is vital for outstanding leaders because it enables them to comprehend and control their feelings while simultaneously establishing a connection with others through empathy. Emotional intelligence is the factor that defines how effectively leaders can negotiate relationships, inspire trust, and encourage their teams. Technical abilities and knowledge are vital, but emotional intelligence makes the difference.

The development of self-awareness enables leaders to understand and control their feelings, preventing them from engaging in conduct that is either impulsive or destructive. In addition, developing empathy allows leaders to comprehend their team members' requirements and worries, leading to improved collaboration and the establishment of robust connections founded on trust, respect, and effective communication.

3.Growth Mindset For All:

Establishing a Growth Mindset environment requires the conviction that applying effort, devotion, and knowledge acquisition can improve one's capabilities and intelligence. The most effective leaders adopt this mentality, realizing that their personal and professional development is not limited but unbounded. They encourage the same mindset among their members to foster learning, innovation, and resilience within their teams. Leaders can create a climate in which individuals feel encouraged to take on challenges, learn from setbacks, and ultimately achieve tremendous success by emphasizing the significance of effort and perseverance rather than intrinsic ability. A culture of continual improvement, a desire to welcome change, and the ability to adapt to new circumstances are all outcomes that can be achieved by cultivating a growth mindset inside a business.

4. Servant Leadership:

Servant leadership is a philosophy that places the success and well-being of the team members ahead of any personal advantages or authority that may be earned. The best leaders know that their first responsibility is to serve their team by providing support and opportunities for growth and development. They make it a point to actively listen to the individuals on their team, value the ideas and perspectives they provide, and give them the tools, resources, and guidance necessary for their success. This method of leadership enables leaders to cultivate strong relationships with their team, encourages a sense of ownership and responsibility, and eventually results in increased levels of team engagement, productivity, and loyalty. Great leaders create a happy and empowering work atmosphere by putting the needs of their team first; this is how they achieve this.

5.Foster Innovation and Creativity:

Great leaders know the significance of cultivating a culture that encourages innovation and creativity within their organization. They inspire their team members to think creatively, ask questions about the current situation, and investigate fresh ideas and potential solutions. Leaders encourage collaboration, inclusion, and a steady stream of fresh ideas by establishing a psychologically secure atmosphere for individuals to feel at ease taking chances and sharing their perspectives. In addition, great leaders acknowledge the significance of varied viewpoints and actively seek out diverse talent. This ensures that various ideas are considered and that decision-making is inclusive, resulting in more innovative and effective solutions.

6. Cultivate and Create a High-Performing Team:

Leadership is not just about the accomplishments of individuals but also about the construction and cultivation of great teams. The best leaders know that a cohesive and well-functioning team can do far more than the sum of the efforts of its members. They put in the time and effort to construct a group of people with abilities that complement one another, different points of view, and similar values. Leaders promote alignment and foster collaboration by providing clear goals, roles, and expectations; this helps to eliminate confusion. Individuals can offer their best work and feel encouraged in their professional development due to their ability to foster effective communication, trust, and psychological safety within the team.

Continuous feedback, coaching, acknowledgment, and the creation of chances for growth and progress are all necessary components in cultivating high-performing teams.

7. Lead Through Complex and Ambiguous Situations:

Outstanding leaders must possess the agility and grace necessary to navigate challenging and ambiguous situations in today's world, characterized by a constantly changing environment. They can make well-informed decisions even when faced with ambiguity because they know no strategy can be applied to every situation.

These leaders adopt a strategic and comprehensive perspective, soliciting feedback from various sources to arrive at well-informed conclusions. They ensure that their decisions are transparent throughout the process and communicate the reasoning behind them in a way that is easy to understand, which builds confidence among their team members. In addition, great leaders maintain a flexible and adaptable mindset, always prepared to adjust their plans and strategies to traverse unforeseen hurdles and grasp opportunities successfully.

8. Practice Ethical Leadership:

Ethics plays a significant role in leadership, as it determines the success of individuals and organizations and their impact on society. Regarding their behaviors and decisions, great leaders prioritize ethical behavior, exhibiting integrity, honesty, and justice in their actions. They are steadfast in their commitment to upholding ethical standards and behave in a manner that benefits their team, stakeholders, and the greater community. Because they are aware that their activities serve as a model for others to emulate, ethical leaders are responsible for their actions and hold themselves accountable. By implementing ethical leadership practices, they can establish trust, cultivate a favorable reputation, and motivate people to behave ethically, thus establishing a culture of excellence within their organization.

9.Leave an Impactful Legacy:

The overarching goal of great leaders is to leave a legacy beyond their accomplishments. It is clear to them that the actual measure of success is not the number of accolades they receive for themselves but rather their influence on the lives of others and the world around them. Through mentoring and providing others with the tools they need to realize their full potential, these leaders are committed to developing future leaders. In addition to promoting diversity and inclusion, they work hard to fulfill their social responsibilities and make a big difference in the communities in which they live.

Great leaders ensure that their influence will continue to be felt long after they have moved on by leaving behind a legacy that includes empowered leaders, sound change, and lasting impact.

Achieving long-term success as a great leader requires embracing lifelong learning, developing emotional intelligence, cultivating a growth mindset, practicing servant leadership, fostering innovation and creativity, building and nurturing high-performing teams, leading through complex and ambiguous situations, practicing ethical leadership, and leaving a legacy of impact.

Exceptional leaders are those who are dedicated to their ongoing development, who can motivate and enable others, and who, through their leadership, make a positive difference in the world.

As we approach the end of our exploration of what it means to become a great leader, let us reflect on the key insights that can guide us on this transformative journey. Outstanding leadership is not just about authority or position; it is about cultivating a deep sense of empathy, an unwavering commitment to integrity, and the ability to inspire and empower those around us. It is about being visionary yet grounded, strong yet compassionate, and decisive yet open to new ideas.

Remember, the path to outstanding leadership is a journey, not a destination. It is a continuous process of learning, growing, and adapting. Embrace every challenge as an opportunity to develop your leadership skills and every success as a chance to uplift and motivate others. Great leaders are not born; they are made through persistent effort, self-reflection, and a steadfast dedication to improving themselves and the lives of those they lead.

As we conclude, let us carry forward the belief that outstanding leadership is within reach of each of us. By being authentic, resilient, and inclusive and nurturing a culture of trust and collaboration, we can all aspire to be leaders who achieve goals and inspire greatness in others. In the words of John Quincy Adams, "If your actions inspire others to dream more, learn more, do more, and become more, you are a leader." Let this be our guiding principle as we strive to unlock the great leader within us.

www.ingramcontent.com/pod-product-compliance
Lightning Source LLC
Chambersburg PA
CBHW082136290526
45794CB00008B/3052